MW01123190

Snow Melts First

in the

Middle of the Slough

Snow Melts First
in the
Middle of the Slough

Catherine J. Stewart

thistledown press

© Catherine J. Stewart, 2019
All rights reserved

No part of this publication may be reproduced or transmitted in any form or by any means, graphic, electronic or mechanical, including photocopying, recording, or any information storage and retrieval system, without permission in writing from the publisher or a licence from The Canadian Copyright Licensing Agency (Access Copyright). For an Access Copyright licence, visit www.accesscopyright.ca or call toll free to 1-800-893-5777.

Thistledown Press Ltd.
410 2nd Ave. North
Saskatoon, Saskatchewan, S7K 2C3
www.thistledownpress.com

Library and Archives Canada Cataloguing in Publication

Title: Snow melts first in the middle of the slough / Catherine J. Stewart.
Names: Stewart, Catherine J., 1959- author.
Description: Poems.
Identifiers: Canadiana 20190063270 | ISBN 9781771871945 (softcover)
Classification: LCC PS8637.T49425 S66 2019 | DDC C811/.6—dc23

Cover photograph by Catherine J. Stewart
Cover and book design by Jackie Forrie
Author photograph by Gerhardt Lepp
Printed and bound in Canada

Thistledown Press gratefully acknowledges the financial support of the Canada Council for the Arts, the Saskatchewan Arts Board, and the Government of Canada for its publishing program.

Contents

Burgess Shale Fossils
— *Field, BC*

Over 500 million years ago
the first immigrants,
permanence in soft bodies,
undulated in an inland sea.

A landslide and their last
breath is mud, its weight
compressing organs
into stone.

They waited millennia
for earth's upheaval,
their tomb split open
to reveal life's tracings,

that last gasp splayed
on cliff face.

Galena

Claim staked in 1883 —
Jubilee Mountain marked,
measured, owned.

For 70 years, Galena ore —
silver, lead, zinc — was clawed
from the mountain, ballast

shipped out of the valley.

Barite, white dust dredged
from the tailings ponds, rose
from ore trucks and settled

into the clothes hanging on the line. We
wore it to school, to basketball games.
We danced in it.

The ducks we plucked
on the hillside, breasts filled
with shot made from Galena ore —

lead finding its way home.

Migration

A mallard lures
his mate with a wingspan's
empty boast and the length
of his outstretched neck.

The pair migrate north to the slough
of her birth where he lingers
hoping to mate again; finally
he absconds with a pintail
while she sits on the nest,
the penance of eggs pressed
against her underbelly.

In the fall the mallard drops
to the slough's surface
but doesn't recognize
his offspring or the scent
of his mate. Flies south
in the same vee but doesn't
draft the wind for her.

Nature's Fury

— St Mark's Church circa 1905

In Sunday white, Lorrine tethered her mare and foal,
sat in a pew beside her parents,
hands folded,
feet still,
eyes
      on the window.

Black clouds darkened the pulpit.

The minister lit a lantern
to his Old World god, paused
when bolts of light ricocheted off his face
and thunder crushed his voice,
bellowed when the electric air
gathered momentum in the pause
preceding the rumble
that shook the church.

Outside the walls, lightning
rent the sky, sacrificed
her horses, found earth.

      She knelt, forehead pressed
      to her foal's muzzle, waited
      for the breath that never came —
      the reminder of rain cold

      on her neck. She pulled off
      her boots and stockings,
      stumbled wildly home
      barefoot
         in the mud.

Inheritance

Lorrine grew up on the Columbia, caught
pikeminnow with too many bones
for eating, stalked a kingfisher
until its dark tunnel in the bank
swallowed its voice, dipped her feet
in the silt-mired water, leaned
face-first into the breath of the lumbering
river, many-tongued wind blowing
off the dimpled surface, and thirsted
for the water she couldn't drink.

When William arrived in the spring
of 1911, on the riverboat,
the motion of the water
in his feet, she thought
he would know the river's
secrets, take her
to its source, that their blood
stirred together would whisper
through their children's veins
like the river
between its banks,
so the children
of their children would feel,
always, the pull
of the river
in their bones.

Immigration

Books boxed, a child's hand in each
of hers, my mother's mother walked backwards

into this country, eyes still reflecting London's
cobbled streets. What could the thin-aired light

offer her? Only pine trees for neighbours
and the Columbia murmuring to itself. Lost

in conversations inside her head, Maude buttered
both sides of the toast, wandered up and down

the stairs while her children's feet chattered
on uneven floorboards, pounded on the river bank

a noisy jubilance. Her leaded crystal broke
by the glass, china shattered, her books wore thin

and ripped at the edges, and her children's nails
dug into the soft fir table. The dry air

cleared London's smog from her lungs so she smoked,
each inhalation drawing her backwards.

Carbonate Landing, BC

Their first home was accessible
only by water, the riverboat inn
deserted fifteen years earlier,
after train tracks were laid
on the other side of the Columbia.

Maude unpacked her books,
read to her children,
read the same stories again
and again, raised her voice
above the wilderness.

Every evening the coyotes'
promises, like the Pied Piper's,
lured her children from their beds,
from the house, until
they dropped on all fours
and entered the woods.
She didn't hear the piping
so couldn't follow.

Orphan

Montana circa 1890

Mother

Her cross swaying
beyond reach

Not Mother

He remembers
the rancher's wife
who raised him

forehead shirred
like his cousin's smock

hair to rival
the dappled grey mare

mother's cross
beneath her stiff lace collar

Mother

Lullaby -
he has an affinity
with mockingbirds

Not Mother

Cold hand on his forehead
checking the night's fever

but the cross
swinging free
a reminder against his cheek

Mother

in a wheat field
he recognized
blondness

Not Mother

She doled out
bread and beans

tasked him to cut a willow switch
the shape of his disobedience

Mother

Not a memory

Not Mother

Her hoarse screams
form the darkness behind him
a runaway at eleven years old
on the dappled grey mare
cross in hand
galloping anywhere

   Spillimacheen circa 1916

When his wife returns to bed
after nursing, nightie scented
with milk, it is his mother
he remembers

The Trapper's Wife

She leans her forehead
against the window,
breath fogging glass.

Steel traps rattling, he strides
away from the house,
snowshoes crushing
mesh prints into snow,
cutting into field
and frozen slough
before he dissolves like a mirage
of willow wood.

In two nights the cold
swirls frozen on the window
and, heavy at the foot of her bed,
stone loses all memory of oven.

Four days in and the bucket clunks
on the ice sheet in the shallow well.
She makes water from snow,
just the woodstove and a battered bucket
that rocks on the hot cast iron.

By dark the coyotes circle the cabin.
High-pitched yelps curl
around the small of her back
and settle in her womb.

By day she searches the hills for smoke,
white wisps threading to the sky,
but there is no lightness rising from the dark
forests, only the silence of trees.

The seventh night black turns white.
For two days the snow erases her
as she walks
to the outhouse
to the barn
to the field.

Ten days now and the cow moos in the barn,
summer in its hay-scented breath,
steam in the milk her frigid hands
coax from its udder.
She leans her head against its side
and the calf's heartbeat taps her forehead.

She returns often to the barn,
stands still, shushed
for the faint rustle of breath
like white silk skirts at a wedding.

Trapper's Curse

On the second day out,
twenty miles along his trap line
an emptied trap, steel jaws
bloodied, tufts of fur,
remnants of marten.

When mercury freezes, snow
constricts finer than sand, light
as fresh-plucked goose down,
and cold.

Wolverine
Gulo gulo,
skunk bear,
carcajou —

the largest weasel,
fiercest, in deep snow
the shadow of deer and moose.

The trapper sets a wolverine trap
beneath the snow, baits
it with rabbit.

Snow crystals embed between fibres
in wool pants, melt and freeze
in a beard.

Dark brown on top, pale
on the sides, a wolverine's fur
resists frost.

Nightfall, the longest hour,
the trapper returns to his cabin,
lights his airtight stove,

blows warmth back
into his hands.

Another trap has been raided,
the wolverine set sprung.

The trapper sights his gun
into the trees.

There is no movement,
no breath but his,
timed

to his heartbeat.

        White — the colour of breath
        when it freezes.

                Wolverine doesn't cross
                the trapper's path but follows,
                soft pads scuffing webbed
                snowshoe tracks.

The trapper finds emptied traps,
scattered fur, massive paw prints,
doesn't see the thief,
but smells him.

        Whiteout — falling snow
        obscuro.

                Wolverine buries rabbit,
                claims it with musk.

The trapper's cabin gapes
open, doorjamb clawed,
lock hanging.

Inside, overturned shelves,
pans scattered and cans punctured,
beans and Spam sucked out, reek
of wolverine.

The trapper lights a fire,
burns off the stench,
and in the morning
nails the door shut.

                 Snow, a whiteness so intense
                 it can blind a man.

                         Prowling its territory,
                         wolverine scampers
                         over snowshoe trails,
                         follows them to the meal
                         stiffening in a trap,
                         follows on to the cabin's shelter,
                         gnaws its way in.

The trapper ties his gun
from a branch, trigger-rigs
meat and waits for hunger
to lure the wolverine.

Snow falls,
six feet deep,
deeper, obliterates
landmarks, trees,
trapper's cabin,
the way out.

Ode to the Columbia River

Silver thread unspooling
between clay banks
from the source
to the Pacific, now
at Mica Dam —
                    cut off.

Many tongues named this river.
The Ktunaxa, Syilx and Secwepemc
hunted along its banks, European traders
in the SS Columbia Rediva navigated inland
for furs, David Thompson overwintered
in a tent at Boat Encampment, on the bend
where the northward rush turned
south, where traders from the east met traders
from the west and settlers' dreams whispered
across the water sank in eddies. The Big Bend
Highway still snakes below, with silt
like shed skins on old asphalt. A bridge
torn apart no longer connects
a country; an owner dismantled
his Shell station, the hands that built it clumsy
in the unbuilding, nails scattered in the dust.
Here Kinbasket Lake clambered over
the banks to sprawl belly up
in the sun.

Now, river succumbs
to downstream flow, pools
in the purgatory behind concrete walls
where all is mouthed clean
by bottom-feeding catfish.

The Bugaboos

Hound's Tooth, Marmolata, Dogpatch, Howser Spire, Pigeon,
Crescent, Eastpost, Northpost, and Bugaboo — a miner's dead-
end, thwarted golden promise of iron pyrite, empty tunnels into
mountains.

Conrad Kain was first to unravel
symmetry of rock and crevice,
to scale the summit before clouds
closed in and forced retreat.

Bugaboo — a climber's nightmare of falling rock, white out,
freezing rain.

In 1948 lightning electrified cave
walls, seared climbers denied the summit,
Rolf Pundt twitched to the edge, disappeared
into the abyss.

Bugaboo — a bugbear, imagined or real defeat.

Cars at the Bugaboo trailhead wrapped
in chicken wire, rocks and posts.

A porcupine will chew through hoses
and brake lines, gnaw on tires,
lumber off.

Bugaboo — a bogie, mountain spirit sequestered in crevasse
or rock cleft.

Wind, a snow-wraith
swirling from peak to peak,
on guard, restless.

Chambermaid, Golden Lodge Hotel Circa 1930

Her day off, Mary breaks a sprig of lilac from the hotel bush. Puts it in a glass on the window sill in her room. Then she removes her coat from the hanger, lays it across the grey wool blanket on her narrow bed. The hanger's thin metal bends easily in her hands. She twists it apart, straightens the curves and places it on the washstand beside the basin. The water is cold but she wets her washcloth anyway, rubs the bar of soap over the thin fabric. Cleans the hanger with it. The sharp end of the metal snags her finger, draws blood. She wipes the metal again, balances it across the basin and wraps the cloth around her finger. Then she spreads her towel on the floor and removes her dress, her stockings, her briefs. Drapes them across her coat. She settles on the towel, leans against the wall, and reaches for the hanger. It is the lilac she looks at. The surprise of purple framed by grey sky.

My Father's Gift to My Mother

He laid a dead duck at your feet. And you — a vegetarian.

Then he left you alone with it. Flopped on the floor — belly up,
neck twisted, beak back, orange webbing just touching the tip
of your brown shoe. Dead. You knew what you had to do. Bend
over, grasp the emerald head. Smell the gunpowder, the spent
barrel of the shotgun.

Outside you clutch the feet with one hand and there on top of
the bank, feathers fly. And you pluck the down to pallid goose-
pimpled flesh darkly spotted with pinfeathers. Drumsticks and
naked wings cold. Still. Its head in your hand. Clouded eyes right
there. And you lay that neck on your chopping block, drop the
sharp blade of the axe down through the pale ring encircling its
throat. Then your knife. You slice the skin, jagged slit spilling
the offal, blood red in the white enamel bowl. Is that when you
know all his gifts will be impossible?

You use Saskatoon branches to start a fire, there on the frozen
grass, the bitter green wood smoking into the meat as you singe
the pinfeathers. Your cold, red hands warmed by the flames.

In the house, you stuff the hollow cavity with bread, celery,
onions, sage, food you like disappearing into that dark space.
And it scents the house, the fat sizzling in the roaster.

They come in, him and his buddies with their beer, to sit around
the table. And you are lost in the Spitfire spiralling down into
the Channel with the Irish boy you loved, as you chop potatoes
over the pot on the wood stove and bend around the men to set
out the plates.

Out of Season

My father squats behind the willow, rifle to his shoulder, squints his left eye shut and with his right stares through the sight down the barrel to the deer on the gravel bar. Behind him, his sister's three skinny kids crouch. The little girl slaps at a mosquito and the deer's head flicks up. My father scowls but doesn't shift his gaze. He focuses on the deer. It's nearer now. His finger tightens on the trigger and the slug barrels into the animal's chest. The deer lurches forward, knees falter, collapses.

He skins, guts and quarters the animal. Splays it out. Sere white membrane taut over the red-blue flesh, the broad spread of the haunches and thin legs. Dark hooves. He wipes away blood with its hide. Nothing to drip, leave a trail back to the house. He washes his hands in the river, glances at the remains. Food for coyotes. Then he gives the oldest boy a front quarter and the youngest boy a hind. The girl clutches the wild tiger lilies she has picked for her mother and holds out her arms for her piece. The hind quarter is almost as big as she is and she crushes the orange petals against the red meat. My father slings his gun onto his shoulder, lifts the last quarter.

The light is fading as they walk the mile down the railroad track. Mosquitoes follow them, sting the girl's bare legs, her arms. She can't swat them, just trudges down the tracks. The broken orange heads fall from the lilies, piece by piece, every time she shifts her grip on the deer. The meat is warm in her hands. When she has to rest, my father makes her sit on the rail with the deer on her lap, off the ground. She squirms her skirt down so the bare meat doesn't touch her skin. Bats flicker over the sloughs, the last reflected daylight. Ahead, the house lights are on.

Trains

Before the rooster, the train
shuddered the house awake
a hundred feet
from the tracks.

Coal trains from Fernie,
black smears along the river,
an echo down the valley
between the Rockies and Purcells.

It was a wheat train that derailed
on the corner by my aunt's house,
broken red cars disgorging gold
over the coal dust. We came
with our gunny sacks,
my parents, brother, sisters,
my aunt and her kids,
second cousins. We came to the heat
of the sun, the itch of chaff,
the soft slur of kernels sliding
from scoop to sack.

For years afterwards the trains slowed
before that corner and my cousins
ran alongside,
their worn sneakers slapping
the stony rail bed,
then airborne they scrabbled
for a grip on the box-car ladders.
For a moment
        they could go anywhere.

Mountain Huckleberries

The blue hill. Eighteen miles up
the Bugaboo Road. A short descent
of the bank and   huckleberries.
Fat as the top of my father's
thumb. But the race is on. From the first
plonk of berry on tin — no tasting.

Parents, aunt, siblings, cousins
squat into their picking. Disappear
in the patch.

My sister steps on a wasp nest, anger
curls around her legs, chases
her, while branches slap against
face, arms, thighs, and berries
bounce from her pail. My father
plasters Bugaboo mud
on her fiery skin.

Chameleons we change.
Purple hands. Purple
teeth. Purple tongues.

Our bucket contents are scanty,
chaotic with twigs and leaves
while father, with no guilty stains,
carries two pails burgeoning with berries.
Shiny, black, succulent.

Father

I watch old Humphrey Bogart movies cause he reminds me of
you. Gruff jawed. Bristle chinned. Lined. The high forehead.
The hair swept up and back. Stoop shouldered. Sparse bodied. I
search the movies for your redeeming features.

Humphrey in the Sierra Madres. The hard work. The sweat.
The dirt. Dust in your hair. You slept with it and woke with it. I
never saw you step into the small enamel tub that Mum would
place behind the wood cook stove and shroud with blankets.
Like getting into a coffin and hot like hell. Though you had no
trouble entering the bar, like Rick in Casablanca.

Eddie was the first of us kids to wait alone in the truck. To have
to drive you home. In the winter. How long did he sit in the cold
and the dark each time? At 17 he blew like a sawed-off shotgun.
Wouldn't stop. Couldn't stop. Not 'til he banged you up against
the chimney and knocked it askew and Mum had to come
running with the oven mitts on to set it straight. The airtight
heater, red fire in its belly. Spitting and crackling.

Your African Queen, your Rose. Mum got bladder cancer. From
your three-pack-a-day habit. The car cumbrous with smoke
and us all choking on it. Cigarette dangling from your mouth.
Bogarted. Exhalations shared. But your last gift didn't kill her.
She wouldn't join you in your grave. Finally stubborn.

I avoided looking at your hands. They were stubby cigarette-
stained black-behind-the-nail hands. Careless cold-to-the-touch
callused hands. Bitter beer-hardened hands. There wasn't one
good thing about them.

Apples

Eddie was six years old,
out with his father, just the two guys
picking apples.

The black surprise of dew
on his brown leather shoes,
the leaf-gold ground,
the shiny tin pails overflowing.
How round and red the apples,
how sweet. He remembers

on the way home they stopped
at the Golden Arms Hotel,
"just for a minute," but he waited so long
that he had to pee and went inside
to the bathroom in the lobby
next to the bar.

Looking out the window he saw
five older boys in the truck-bed
shoving apples in their pockets.

He pounded on the door of the bar
'til someone came and fetched his father.
He pointed to the truck, begged
to go home. But behind the door
there was still beer in his father's glass,
a cigarette in the ashtray,

so he sat alone in the truck with cold
hands and feet, the buckets in the back
and the apples —
small and scabbed
and few.

In the Parking Lot Outside the Bar

Dirty ankles, third-hand shoes and a day so hot spit evaporated
    before it hit the ground.
We rode dust horses around the parking lot, my two sisters and I,
    English style, jumped potholes, make-believe fences.
Named into being they were prancing and fearless,
    they were dappled and they were light.

We went all day without food or drink, but our horses dipped
    their nostrils in our imaginary streams;
they ate the dry grass green and galloped, their manes
    and their tails like air.

After dark we didn't ride the horses because they might trip
    on the potholes in the parking lot
and they were so tired they turned back to dust.

After dark we sat in the truck.

Father, Tell Me Our Lie Again

Show me that your hands
are steady on the wheel.

Father I'm lying
on the truck seat
out of view
as my friends drive by.

I count to ten and ten
and ten hundred
but you don't find me
until I've forgotten
to count.

Slouched into your body,
you smell of beer and smoke,
the bar slur ponderous
on your tongue.

Your hands steady,
not an alcoholic's.

Tell me again.

Is an alcoholic the man who drinks
to oblivion or the man who is oblivious
while he drinks?

His daughter watches daylight
collapse into dusk, into dark,
eight hours in the cab,
learning it's useless to count
on anything.

His Hands

i

His first touch twinned,
four hands in amniotic water,
then to live with two.

ii

In Spillimacheen no school
after grade eight. He trades his pen
for railway ties, creosote stains.

iii

A snowstorm, his wife in labour,
car stuck on the roadside:
his useless hands, his strangled child.

iv

A bumper crop, potatoes
pulled from the dirt, frozen
in the root house he built.

v

He cuts dovetails in logs,
a home for his wife, but still
the cold finds them.

vi

He reaches for refuge
in the quiet of her body
then his hands fold together,
trembling on the pillow.

High Water

In 1968 we moved to the west side of the Columbia, to my
grandparents' abandoned farm. Rats had usurped the farmhouse
and the lower fields slouched into the slough. The broken
hand-pump on the well coughed up air.

> Washout Creek tumbles
> past our old house. Fresh
> drinkable water.

> The first rush of spring and dawn
> resplendent with mosquito-winged
> prisms. The house vibrates
> with their high-pitched whine.

We hauled our drinking water from Washout in a five-gallon
galvanized can. Mother packed washing water from the slough,
bailing it into two metal buckets which she lugged up the clay
bank and set on the cookstove to heat.

> The Columbia churns with spring
> melt — silt-sullied, undrinkable — swells
> over its banks.

Mother drove the old pickup, five of us in the cab, into the flood
which poured under the truck doors onto the floorboards. A
glut of water. Our feet on the seat. Hands steady, she steered the
track the road had worn in her mind.

Tightrope Walkers

My sisters and I were the next Great Blondins,
the board fence our rope,
the pigsty our Niagara.

Eight feet between posts.

We balanced on thin-cut slabs,
farmyard funambulists
inching across, arms

o

u

t

s

t

r

e

t

c

h

e

d

like barn swallow fledglings
on the clothesline, testing
the wind in their feathers.

Hopscotch

Every spring the sun
peeled back the snow,
skinned the dirt road,
a softness we carved into.

We used barrel keys
warmed to our palms
for markers. They landed flat
and didn't skip
over boundaries.

One-legged we hopped
the course, over
boxes, past markers,
all the way to the end
and back home.

But my brother drew a moon so big
only he could leap across.

Pig Summer

Morley Wells sold us forty pigs,
thirty-nine sows and one boar.
Pigs, pigs a passel of pigs —
pink ones, rust ones,
some with black spots,
pregnant sows
and that one boar.

Soon sows were farrowing
one after the other,
eight ten twelve piglets each
hungry piglets suck suck sucking
squealing grunting greedily slurping
butting out the runts,
scrawny curlytailed runts.

Runts in boxes on the oven door
nursed black rubber nipples
on pop bottles.

Freerange pigs —
the boar the sows all those piglets
trotted up the driveway,
rooted in the flower bed,
paraded on the porch.

Dick   Fringey Ears   Saddleback
Granny   Daffy   Curly Toes
Tamie   Bossy   Long Nose
Tippie Toes   and   Butcher!

Why would a kid name her pet pig Butcher?

Inoculation time
a cousin picked a piglet up by the belly!
Father ran around and around the truck,
Bossy grunted behind,
my sisters and I inside the cab yelled,
Run Daddy run!

She caught him when he leapt into the back,
his arm between her teeth but she let go.
He always said it was because she knew him.

Midafternoon in the heat
Butcher and I
asleep in the shade
a pig for a pillow
and a pillow for a pig
pig limbs person limbs
akitter and akimbo
pigtapestry

Pigs in the house
with flour-dusted snouts
white hoofprints down the hall

Pigs for sale

Weaner pigs in gunny sacks
happy pigs rooting at the scent of potatoes
into the trunk   gone

Five minutes later
a knock at the door
the two men standing there
dripping wet
their car in the channel
the pigs still in the trunk

still in their gunny sacks
and the car full of water

Where the tap drips — mud
muckinable mud
skin cakeable mud
flyproof pigs

Where the tap drips
my sister and I rolling
slippery squishy mud-smeared people pigs

Sows wheeling and squealing
we astride them
one two three of us
pigrodeo

Fall and the forty-five gallon barrel of water,
a fire burning below,
three pine poles teepeed above
and a huge iron hook dangling in the steam.

Butcher and I
along the field
down the bank
fingers crossed hooves crossed
just to make it through this one day
but they found us.

I always knew they would.

Heatwave

By noon the ground like a second
sun cooked the soles of our feet,
forced us onto the raft.

Our toes amongst hollow reeds
found cool-bodied leeches.

By late afternoon the air
grumbled, dark clouds stalked
the mountains, hovered.

My sisters and I in our swimsuits,
a dervish of arms and legs,
calloused feet drumming
the ground until

a brief pelting of hailstones
melted in our hair
and smashed the morning glory
before it bloomed.

Summer's End

In late August the pigsty simmered with flies.
The wallows, dry and lumpy, offered no solace,
pigs lolled in the shade, panting.

I sprawled beside Butcher, right arm
across his fattened belly, half oblivious
to buzzing flies and his skin that flinched
as they landed, and lost to daydreams

of Butcher still a curly-tailed runt
in the farmyard again green and growing
as he snuffled for roots and mucked
in the full, wet wallows. I slept.

Heat gathered in the day's frayed edges,
collected cumulusly over the pasture.

A Good Year for Mushrooms

After a dry summer,
the rain.

Thirst is mycelia,
sere and curled
inward.

> In 1975, my family hiked to the Lake of the Hanging
> Glacier. Cigarettes blurred Father's lungs.

With water, fungal hyphae
blossom into honey
mushrooms, largest
of living organisms,
an underground network
tangled with roots,
killing maples in a bitter
saprophytic love.

> The lake trail zigzagged uphill, leaned
> into steepness, an eight-hundred-metre gain.
> Breath constricted.

A good year and the *Marasmius*
stand en pointe, tutus ruffled
in the wind; shy amanitas hide
under lacy veils and dead
leaves; *Helvella vespertina*:
earth's eruption.

> Father lagged and I, too, paused
> on the corners, turned over leaves
>   for mushrooms.

Parallax

We lived on the river's west
a mile from our neighbours
with no god to pray to,

only the advent of geese,
a new season.
First frost

shivered in the power
lines blurring our southern view,
        murmured to wing

beat, that ecstasy
of air and feathers —
flight. We never knew

where they went,
one day in the sloughs,
the next in the sky
and diminishing.

On the Way to the School Bus Stop

Broadside on the gravel road,
black hump hunched against the cold,
a bull moose.

Mother fishtailed the truck.

An impact would hurtle
his thousand pounds across the hood,
shatter the windshield,
crush us all.

Our lights reflected his bulk,
spotlit his bell and breath,
his six-foot antler halo.

Long legs barred the road
'til dawn in its creeping
swallowed the mist, stirred flies,
warmed that cold hump.

When we got to the stop
the bus was gone.

Ode to the Outhouse

My sister and I raced down the hill,
perched side by side

in its auditorium; mosquitoes piped,
flies kazooed,

spring peepers peeped
night's constant chorus,

and all those stars!

A black hornet stung
my bum in its exit,

the Valley Echo's newsprint held
more than the Eaton's catalogue.

    A two-seater,
        one hole large, one small,

        never painted, its boards greyed
        like a wasp's paper nest,

        overturned at Halloween,
        it could always be righted.

We skated in worn shoes
down the slope to its door,

Mum poured ash on the path:
our grip on ice;

once at 20 below my sister waited
for paper,

it took us half an hour
to miss her;

too cold to hold a book
we parsed our exhalations.

Only night knew our dash
through darkness home.

      After the new house rose beside the old,
      solid, heated, plumbed,

      the outhouse became ash
      on Halloween;

      tucked in bed we never saw
      the last sparks ascend.

Ghazal

A fencepost in winter waits
to doff its white hat to the wind.

Once I sang in my sleep, a red-throated
lily briefly unfurled: a shiver of scent.

It's snowing again, muted
flakes obscuring the light.

My cough rasps like a raven
hoarse from squawking.

Snow melts first in the middle
of the slough: an indrawn breath.

Backbone

Maiasaura — a duck-billed dinosaur

It was always there, ossified nubbles protruding,
handholds in a sandstone bank. Large enough
to cast a shadow, small enough
to be ignored.

Lower in the bank a seam of clay moist
and cool in our fingers. Our tarnished spoons
carved caves, silky-smooth clay homes,
molded tables, chairs, beds for our trolls.
Atop the bank our house overrun by hops,
vines snarled around curtainless windows
dislodging faded cedar shingles, inside
a fire in the black bulk of the McClary stove
and a round steak stew, murmuring hot.

Ornithopod bird-hipped, bipedal grazer. Muscled thighs the size
of trees. Footfalls pounding horsetail ferns to shreds. Thirty feet
long, solid meat outpacing the carnivore.

We balanced on the stones, five of them,
three inches wide, the drop
eight feet to the path below.

The path zagged down the bank
into the slough, that open pool
where water could be scooped
into buckets, one for each
hand, the water splashing
over the rims, dark circles in the dust.

Maiasaura. Mother lizard. Four tons perched on triple toes next
the earthen mound that was her nest, layering leaves and eggs

together, compost incubator. Forty eggs. Forty babies. Mother
feeding game-legged hatchlings, duck-bill slipping across their
cheeks.

The quiet house in winter, the linden stripped,
birches barren. Our mother at the clothesline
grappling with stiff, frozen sheets.

Hatchlings, forty hatchlings, tottering then strong, bursting out
of the nest, running, running, gone. Giant empty bowl speckled
with eggshell remains. Maiasaura snuffling in the dirt, eyes on
the horizon, calling.

Our mother entered the walking race determined
to never break stride unlike the cheaters
who ran, undetected, in the woods.

Huge hadrosaur, defiant to the end, lumbering, dragging her
tired bulk along the river bank, bony spine stretched to wedge-
tail tip. All that back-ended ballast defying gravity. What
brought her down? T-Rex? Velociraptor? A broken leg?

They came to carve her backbone from the bank
with their shovels and brushes, their jackhammers,
winches and slings, fenced chicken wire
around the hole they'd plunged into her rocky bed.

Beneath the house, ear pressed to rock,
I heard the tap, tap, tap of their hammers and chisels,
leaned into the cold. Maiasaura wrested from her earth
with groan of block against block and hoisted
onto the back of the waiting truck.

As darkness falls over brindle-
scarred sandstone and curtainless windows,
a cricket chirps.

Lotare and Keefair

Childhood gods sculpted from slough
water, wintergreen and the song
of the red-winged blackbird.

In the late afternoon all dozed
except me on my back in the reeds beneath
the sky's changing topography.

No wind rustled birch leaves. No whisper
of snake skin slid between grass stalks. Birdsong
curled up and slept in my ears.

My sun, my moon. My secret worship.
I named them: Lotare and Keefair.

A breeze in my hair returned
movement and I arose
from the soft earth.
No imprint remained.

Sharing Tea

Fragile china cups on the scarred table her grandfather
had built, my mother poured our tea, offered me
an oatmeal cookie, told me, "It was customary among the Inuit,
in winters of want, for the elderly to leave the warmth
of the igloo and wander into day's darkness. To wrap
the cold like a blanket around their bodies, lie
in a snow bed and fall asleep so that their children
and their children's children
might eat."

"When my time comes," she said, "I will answer the call
of the coyotes, walk into a night flush with northern
lights. Make my bed in the tall grass by the slough, let
the mosquitoes hum me to sleep. And there
the river's offspring will find me and claim me
for their own."

The Magpie

One for sorrow/Two for joy/Three for a girl/Four for a boy/
Five for silver/Six for gold/And seven for a secret that's never
been told.
— Anon

"One for sorrow," you once told me,
a clothes peg in one hand,
a wet sheet in the other
and the magpie there
on the roadside, watching.

One magpie, black
beak scrabbling in the gravel,
rises up as a car passes
then returns, rises, returns.
There is no second magpie,
no joy, only grit
that sticks in the beak.

Did you see magpies
before your first child's birth?
The umbilical cord slippery with your blood,
a serpentine collar for her neck,
no breath, no breath.

All sitting on your windowsill,
beaks tapping on the glass.
Or was there only one,
one and the afterbirth.

Years later they came back,
five, to mock you,
your hair the only silver proffered.

Are they with you now, mother,
seven — spectral, sere?
Their secret,
there on the edge of darkness
beyond the window pane.

The wind tangles
in the loose edge of the gutter
and the rain, with nothing to catch it,
falls.

After You're Gone

for my mother

In an attic room,
with the first cool blush of night
and no light on the stairs,
a flitting: attar of the Rugosa rose
sprangled below in your garden,
brazen magenta blooms bursting
from pricked limbs like fireworks.
It's the runaway stallion crashing
through the door of an empty stable,
gone amok in the gardenerless garden
where all else has withered and died.

Passages Through Water

i

The slough's surface fractures
light, story; mosquito-
winged reflections sink.

ii

In the slough at my aunt's farm,
my legs lost in the muck. Water
beetles skitter away.

The itch after swimming,
a second skin —
baby leeches.

Boys held
our heads under.

Water erased
my sister's sight.

She only came to when air
found her lungs.

A dragonfly nymph climbs a reed
out of the water, lets the sun
crack skin, dry wings, destroy
her ability to swim.

iii

Skinny-dipping in the dark,
our two forms a curvature
of night.

Do leeches know
the mad tangle of their bodies,
that brief pleasure before water
washes them apart?

iv

I kayak alone
on west coast waters,
buoyed by the air
trapped inside my boat.

Now that's all
there is, this
surface, no
ocean below.

Toadsong, Spillimacheen

In the slough near
where I was born a fairytale
of foam filled with slick-
tailed tadpoles, a flood,
water bled into the field.

The road dry, pale gravel replete
with bodies dark, wet, risen
from the stagnant water of their birth,
thousands crossing at night,
for a moment bright in the headlights.
Prehistoric in khaki.

Boys would blow them up
through a straw in the anus
then smash them on the bridge.

It is that fetid air, that slough
water in my veins run rampant, ravaging.
It is black tadpole heads and black tadpole tails,
the soft-bodied slither over my bare legs in fomenting water
the curl, the lick. Oh

I am toadlike, risen.

I have left the morass
crossed the road.

Toadsong, toadfoam,
toadgone gone gone.

Where once toad chorus
rumbled day into sleep —
the tongue-tied slough.

Lesson from Poetry Class — Spring 2013
Allow yourself an hour a day to do nothing.

Nothing is that lake where the call of the loon stretches
to the shore, finds the borders
of its space and echoes back; finds its emptiness complete.

Nothing exists in the truck outside the bar where the drumbeat
of a word, any word, broken, repeated, stumbles into cadence —
o-n-o   m-o no
o-n-o-
   m-a
     t-o-
       p-o
        e-i-a
o-n-o-m-a   t-o   p-o-e-i-a
o-n-o-m-a-t-o-p-o-e-i-a
ono
   mato
     poeia
ono mato poeia onomatopoeia onomatopoeia onoonoono
ono
ono
m-a-t-o-p-o-e-i-a — finds the limit of the truck's cab, circles
back like a noose.

Nothing opens the door, lets the flies in.

Messengers

The year after mother's
death, barn swallows
return, the last nest
less than a memory
amidst the ashes
of the old house
thirty years gone.

They dip and lilt over spring
green, cobalt shoulders
flashing, alight
on verandah beams,
beaks full of mud,
for curved nests.

From the window
I try to decipher
her message,
the calligraphy
forked tails etch
into the sky.

Poplars

Every spring, cottonwood sap thickened the air, rose above
the pigsty, above the stench of melting manure, honeyed

promise of copper leaves unfurling into green. Cottonwood
fluff floated past the clothesline, caught on Saskatoon twigs,

tangled in my hair, drifted beyond tree memory, farmyard
boundaries. All summer long the song of ovate leaves

lisping in the heat slipped through the window's screen,
lulled me to sleep, while outside, in the darkness,

seeds sprouted on the wrong side of the fence,
pale roots stunted in the gravel roadbed.

Years later, far beyond the farm, I find them one by one,
map poplars, so every spring I can walk haloed

by sap-scent, dusted by fluff, close my eyes
and breathe myself home.

The Weight of a Moth

There is a graveyard in Ireland on the edge of the village. On the windless side of a sidhe. It is said that on samhain the trapped spirits escape, mingle with the fog. This is the place where at nightfall the corvid crooks its head and tries to sleep, but keeps one eye open. One yellow eye turned to the crack in the hill.

oxygen surrounds the body
drawn in
it carves a pathway to the heart

Fall 1997. Mother steps off the bus onto cobbled streets of shadowed stone. Almost weightless, a moth drifts towards the glow of one amber light smeared by evening fog. Fans its wings to the heat of the bulb. Alights. Burns its tarsi. Rises. Alights again only to burn again and rise again. Over and over the moth succumbs to the taste of fire.

at high altitudes the air
slips thinly
through the teeth

She came to Ireland because of her dream. At seventy, widowed again, she'd opened her cedar chest, found his picture, the Irish boy in uniform, among old papers and placed it on her bedside table. That night in her dream she'd seen the lichen etched on his headstone. A map that showed the way.

Moths without mouths, taste with their tarsi. Touch their hunger.

June 1945. To fly. All he'd ever wanted was to forge his image on the sky, the air buoyant beneath him. To have wings. In his Spitfire to become the hawk spiralling down on its prey. To breathe pure air. Someone forgot to fill his oxygen tank.

deprived of oxygen —
the throat,
a soundless reed

The moth's multi-chambered heart runs the length of its body. So many cavities in which to hide love.

In the hazy shadows below the bulb — a door. His sister's door. She raises her hand. Knocks. The moth beats against the light.

What Can't Be Held

A carved stick waits in my Tibetan
prayer bowl. When I rub it round
the rim — the hum of monks.

The bowl I dropped after
my husband left, a crack fracturing
its surface, leaks red
on my yellow tablecloth.

On my coffee table a bowl woven
from Andean grasses. In it — my talking
stick from Cortez island, glass bottles
from the long-abandoned dump
in Spillimacheen, two eagle feathers
and an empty bird's nest from the larch
tree my daughter and I planted.

Before she comes I set out
my blue porcelain bowl, wash
seven ripe peaches, one for each
day of her visit, and carefully
lay them inside.

The bowl's still there
in the middle of my dining room table
but all the fruit is gone.

Visitor

Spillimacheen 2016

I'm back stumbling in the woods,
plagued by cobwebs.

Twist a bulrush free of its mooring
hold it high and seeds scatter.

The slough grass parts
but when I reach the road and look back
it's closed behind me

as though I was never there.

ACKNOWLEDGEMENTS

For my mother and father

Thank you to my family without whom these poems wouldn't have existed.

Thank you to *Grain* magazine; "Galena" and "My Father's Gift to My Mother" first appeared in issue 41-1. Thank you to Rilla Friesen for nominating these poems for the 2013 National Magazine Awards.

Thank you to *untethered*; "Apples" and "Trains" appeared in the issue Winter 2016.

Thank you to the League of Canadian Poets for posting "The Trapper's Wife" in their newsletter December 2016 and publishing "Poplars" in *Heartwood: Poems for the Love of Trees*, 2018.

Thank you to *Room* magazine; "Migration I", "Immigration" and "Carbonate Landing" appeared in issue 40.3.

Thank you to *Dalhousie Review*; "Parallax" appeared in Vol. 97 No. 3.

Thanks to Tim Lilburn for the epigraph in "Lesson From Poetry Class".

A huge thank you to Michael Kenyon whose insightful editing helped nudge this book into its final state.

I am especially grateful to Lesley Kenny, the first editor of many of these poems, whose encouragement was invaluable.

Thank you for your expert advice: Susan Musgrave, Rhea Tregebov, Karen Solie, George Murray, Brian Brett, Tim Lilburn, Lorna Crozier, Jan Zwicky, Don McKay, and Melanie Siebert.

And thank you to everyone else who lent their eyes and ears to the work in progress including: Jessica Payne, Natalie Rice, Genevieve Lehr, Karina Younk, Gerhardt Lepp, Tanja Saari Bartel, Jann Everard and everyone in my myriad of writing classes.